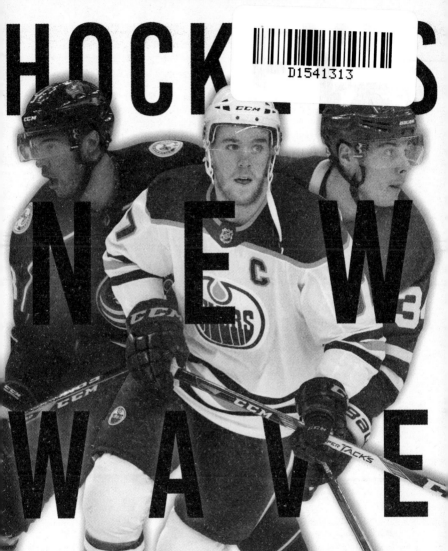

RISING STARS

HOCKEYS

NEW

WAVE

THE YOUNG SUPERSTARS
TAKING OVER THE GAME

CHRIS PETERS

First Edition
First Printing, 2019

Book design by Sarah Taplin
Cover design by Sarah Taplin
Photographs ©: Jay LaPrete/AP Images, cover (left), 48, 121 (top right); Larry MacDougal/AP Images, cover (center); Julian Avram/Icon Sportswire/AP Images, cover (right); Derek Cain/Icon Sportswire/AP Images, 4; Jim Mone/AP Images, 8; Jerome Davis/Icon Sportswire/AP Images, 12, 121 (top left); Danny Murphy/Icon Sportswire/AP Images, 18; Gary Wiepert/AP Images, 22; Chris O'Meara/AP Images, 26, 72; Mike Carlson/AP Images, 30; Julio Cortez/AP Images, 34, 121 (bottom right); Trevor Hagan/The Canadian Press/AP Images, 40; Karl B DeBlaker/AP Images, 44; Adam Lacy/Icon Sportswire/AP Images, 53; Steve Roberts/Cal Sport Media/AP Images, 56, 121 (bottom left); John Woods/The Canadian Press/AP Images, 61; David Zalubowski/AP Images, 64; Russell Lansford/Icon Sportswire/AP Images, 68-69; Chris Young/The Canadian Press/AP Images, 76; Fred Kfoury III/Icon Sportswire/AP Images, 80, 84, 108; Michael Owen Baker/AP Images, 88, 121 (bottom center); Jason Franson/The Canadian Press/AP Images, 94; Jeanine Leech/Icon Sportswire/AP Images, 96, 121 (top center); Mark Humphrey/AP Images, 98-99, 118; Roy K. Miller/Icon Sportswire/AP Images, 104; David Berding/Icon Sportswire/AP Images, 112

Design Elements ©: Shutterstock

Press Box Books, an imprint of Press Room Editions.

Library of Congress Control Number: 2018952200

ISBN
978-1-63494-053-5 (paperback)
978-1-63494-065-8 (epub)
978-1-63494-077-1 (hosted ebook)

Distributed by North Star Editions, Inc.
2297 Waters Drive
Mendota Heights, MN 55120
www.northstareditions.com
Printed in the United States of America

TABLE OF CONTENTS

CHAPTER 1

BROCK BOESER

Every kid who grows up playing hockey in the state of Minnesota dreams of playing at the Xcel Energy Center one day. Most of them hope it's with their high school team playing in the state tournament. However, a select few experience the arena at an even greater level, playing with or against the Minnesota Wild as a National Hockey League (NHL) player.

Brock Boeser was one of those few. In fact, the Burnsville, Minnesota, native got to make his NHL debut in his home state, in front of many friends and family, as part of an extraordinary night.

The amazing run of events began on March 24, 2017. That night, Boeser's sophomore season at the University of North Dakota ended in a tough double-overtime playoff loss in the first round of

Brock Boeser has proven to be a lethal scorer since first joining the Vancouver Canucks in March 2017.

the National Collegiate Athletic Association (NCAA) tournament. The next morning, he signed with the Vancouver Canucks. Hours later, the 20-year-old was dressing with his new Canucks teammates in the visitors' locker room at the Xcel Energy Center. Talk about a whirlwind of 24 hours.

To make a special night even better, Canucks coach Willie Desjardins came up with an especially nice touch. Instead of reading the starting lineup himself, as he usually did, Desjardins invited Brock's parents into the dressing room to announce the team. The surprise gesture was intended to create a memory for the family while also reminding his players of the importance of their own parents in helping them get to where they are.

Brock's parents started reading off the names on the sheet. When they got to the forwards, Brock's mom, Laurie, announced Daniel Sedin as the left wing and Henrik Sedin as center. Then Brock's dad, Duke, took it home.

"And starting on right wing—I can't believe it—Brock Boeser," Duke read.

"I had a few tears in my eyes when they brought them in," Brock said after the game. "I'm thankful for everything they've done for me. Being able to see them before the game was definitely nice. I was really happy to make them proud."

Not only did he make them proud, he gave all of his supporters in attendance—including many family members, friends, and even some of his North Dakota teammates—good reason to cheer loudly.

Halfway through the second period, with the Canucks already leading 2–0, Boeser jammed home a rebound off teammate Bo Horvat's shot for his first NHL goal in his first NHL game. That goal ended up being the game winner, as Vancouver held off Boeser's

ON YOUR 6

Every time Boeser hits the ice with the Vancouver Canucks he wears the No. 6 on his back to keep alive the memory of a close friend. In August 2016, while Brock was playing for Team USA at a youth tournament in Europe, four of his close friends from high school were involved in a terrible car crash. Boeser's former baseball teammate, Ty Alyea, was killed. Alyea wore No. 6 on his baseball jersey. As Boeser found out the night of his NHL debut, No. 6 was also the number his father, Duke, wore in high school. As long as Boeser is a Canuck, that will be his number, too.

Boeser scored his first NHL goal in his home state in front of friends and family as his Canucks beat the Minnesota Wild.

hometown Wild 4–2. It was the perfect way to cap an incredible night for Boeser and his family.

But that was only the beginning. Boeser played in eight more games with the Canucks at the end of the 2016–17 season and added three more goals. He made the NHL look easy, practically.

The following year, Boeser showed that he was not only a flash in the pan. He scored 29 goals and had 55 points in 62 games in his first NHL season. Even though Boeser missed 20 games that season due to an injury, he finished tied with the legendary Daniel Sedin for the team's scoring lead. Boeser also finished second in the voting for the Calder Memorial Trophy given to the league's top rookie.

One of the real highlights of Boeser's first full season in the NHL came when he was selected for the 2018 NHL All-Star Game. Given his goal-scoring prowess, he was selected to compete in the shooting accuracy event during the skills competition, which puts the top players to the test.

The object of the event is to hit five targets as quickly as possible. Each player is timed. Boeser has always had a great shot thanks to years of repetition. But performing in front of a sold-out Amalie Arena in Tampa Bay, in addition to many people watching from home, was a new kind of pressure. Plus, the 20-year-old's competition included some of the very best goal scorers in the game, including Sidney Crosby, Anze Kopitar, Steven Stamkos, Blake Wheeler, Brad Marchand, and James Neal.

Oddly, it was New Jersey Devils forward Brian Boyle, who wasn't much of a prolific goal scorer, setting the standard with hitting all five targets in 11.626 seconds. When it was Boeser's turn, he calmly skated to the spot and then methodically started hitting targets. He missed about three times, but in 11.136 seconds, Boeser had hit every target. He also shot the puck so hard on his final attempt that he broke the target that was equipped with sensors and LED lights. It was one of the most impressive moments of the entire skills competition. And being able to do it in front of a major TV audience instantly made Boeser a bigger star than he was already becoming.

If that wasn't good enough, though, Boeser finished All-Star weekend by leading the Pacific Division All-Stars to the 3-on-3 tournament title. He was also named the All-Star Game Most Valuable Player (MVP), which won him a car.

"I would have never dreamt of this at any time in my life," he said after the game.

> **"I WOULD HAVE NEVER DREAMT OF THIS AT ANY TIME IN MY LIFE."**
>
> **–BROCK BOESER**

The fact is, though, Boeser has always been a goal scorer. He filled the net plenty while with Burnsville High School in Minnesota. When he moved to the United States Hockey League (USHL) to play for the Waterloo Black Hawks, he led the junior league in goals with 35. In college, Boeser was one of the top goal scorers in the NCAA as a freshman as he helped North Dakota claim the 2016 national title. He had four points himself in the national championship game, which was played in Tampa, just like the All-Star Game he played in.

T. J. Oshie, who played at North Dakota before Boeser and went on to his own successful NHL career, was one of the few people not surprised to see how quickly Boeser adjusted to the NHL and started making an impact.

"He's a great player," Oshie said. "He's one of those players that he just makes good, strong plays. He has a nice hard shot. He seems not to overthink with the puck; he kind of takes it as it goes and sees what's open and makes a play. So, great young kid, good hard worker and obviously lots of talent."

BROCK BOESER AT-A-GLANCE

BIRTHPLACE: Burnsville, Minnesota

BIRTH DATE: February 25, 1997

POSITION: Right Wing

SHOOTS: Right

SIZE: 6'1", 191 pounds

TEAM: Vancouver Canucks

PREVIOUS TEAM: University of North Dakota (NCAA) (2015–17)

DRAFTED BY THE CANUCKS 23RD OVERALL IN 2015

CHAPTER 2

RASMUS DAHLIN

Before Rasmus Dahlin ever stepped foot on NHL ice, before he was even drafted by the Buffalo Sabres first overall in 2018, the entire hockey world knew all about this remarkable teenager from Trollhattan, Sweden.

It was March 2017 when the hockey world's attention turned sharply to Dahlin, then only 16 years old. Scouts had been saying he was probably going to be the No. 1 prospect for the 2018 NHL Entry Draft. However, the draft was still a year away and a lot could happen. Needless to say, Dahlin didn't disappoint.

One play during the Frolunda Indians' Swedish Hockey League (SHL) playoffs showed just what he could do. Frolunda trailed rival Skelleftea three games to one in the series. Game 5 was still scoreless when Dahlin took a pass in his own zone. Most defensemen,

A teenage star in Sweden, Rasmus Dahlin joined the Buffalo Sabres as the top pick in the 2018 NHL draft.

especially young ones, would be looking to pass. But Dahlin noticed he had some open ice if he could shake the oncoming forward. Dahlin turned the puck up the ice, then cut to the middle and found himself with a lot of room. He slipped past another Skelleftea forward and drifted to the other side of the ice. At that point, he had two opposing players closing in and he was losing room fast.

That's when Dahlin pulled a beautiful move to the inside, splitting the Skelleftea players and getting himself some open ice in the offensive zone. There was one more player to beat. Dahlin beat him easily with a quick move before firing a wrist shot past the goaltender. The Frolunda fans went into a frenzy. The 16-year-old Dahlin got a standing ovation from the sold-out crowd in Frolunda's stadium in Gothenburg, Sweden. No one could believe what they just saw.

Later, Dahlin said that he kind of blacked out during the play and couldn't quite remember it. All he knew was that it was a good result, and that was enough for him. Amazingly, Frolunda managed to come back from the 3–1 series deficit to beat Skelleftea in seven games. The spark for that comeback was lit by their incomparable teenage defenseman.

From that moment on, everyone in the hockey world knew who Rasmus Dahlin was. If he could make plays like that against professionals at such a young age, surely he was going to be the No. 1 pick in 2018. But he still had an entire season to get through before he could be drafted into the NHL.

Dahlin continued to wow fans in the SHL rinks for another year. He finished with 20 points, the second most points in a SHL season by a U18 player. Considering how many NHL greats played in the SHL as teenagers—players such as Peter Forsberg, Markus Naslund, Henrik and Daniel Sedin, and many more—it says a lot that Dahlin had one of the most productive seasons ever by a 17-year-old, especially because he's a defenseman.

During his draft season, Dahlin also starred for Team Sweden. First, he helped Sweden win a silver medal at the 2018 World Junior Championship. Competing on his future home ice in Buffalo, Dahlin was named the U20 tournament's best defenseman despite being one of the youngest players there. A few weeks later, he was the youngest men's hockey player period at the Olympic Winter Games in PyeongChang, South Korea.

There are a lot of things that make Dahlin special among defensemen, but as that highlight reel goal against Skelleftea showed, he's one of the more creative puck handlers. He can see the ice incredibly well and has tremendous anticipation. This helps him make quick decisions and find seams in the ice where defenders can't get to him.

Hakan Andersson had a chance to see Dahlin up close as a member of Frolunda's board of directors.

INSPIRED BY LIDSTRÖM

Many great Swedish defensemen have played in the NHL. Nicklas Lidström stands above the rest. The other Swedish defensemen often credit Lidström as their inspiration, and for good reason. Before Lidström, no European defenseman—let alone a Swedish one—had won the Norris Trophy. Lidström won it seven times. Since then Erik Karlsson and Victor Hedman have been Swedes to collect the top prize for defenders. It's a trend that could continue with Dahlin and others. Says Lidström of the Swedish defenders in the league: "They're all playing with their heads up. They're trying to be creative. They're all strong skaters. They can join the rush. They can be part of the offense, and they're really solid in their own zone too."

"He's good at everything," Andersson told the *Detroit Free Press*. "He has great size, he is a great skater, he has very good hands. He's extremely smart, and he has very high dedication. There is a lot to like."

There was a lot to like for the Sabres. With Dahlin on the blue line and young forward Jack Eichel up front, the team believes it has its two cornerstones for a generation to come. Dahlin, for his part, couldn't wait to get started.

"It's an amazing feeling. To actually put on this jersey, this logo is amazing," Dahlin said during his introductory press conference in Buffalo. "I've been waiting for this for so long. Finally I'm here."

RASMUS DAHLIN AT-A-GLANCE

BIRTHPLACE: Trollhattan, Sweden
BIRTH DATE: April 13, 2000
POSITION: Defense
SHOOTS: Left
SIZE: 6'2", 185 pounds
TEAM: Buffalo Sabres
PREVIOUS TEAM: Frolunda (SHL) (2016–18)
DRAFTED BY THE SABRES FIRST OVERALL IN 2018

CHAPTER 3

JACK EICHEL

When Jack Eichel arrived on the campus of Boston University in 2014, fans already knew the Terriers had landed a special player. Scouts had projected Eichel to be the kind of player who could change an NHL team's fortunes. He had all of the tools to become a star—good size, powerful skating, high-end puck skills, and an advanced hockey mind. It was a foregone conclusion that he would go first or second in the 2015 draft. The only question was whether Eichel, or Canadian Connor McDavid, would go first.

Even knowing all of that, no one quite expected Eichel to put together one of the best seasons by a freshman in college hockey history. But that's just what he did.

Jack Eichel is part of a promising young core of Buffalo Sabres.

BU is traditionally one of college hockey's great programs. The school is also not far from Eichel's hometown of North Chelmsford, Massachusetts. Those factors made his arrival all the more anticipated. And in his one and only season at BU, Eichel dropped jaws in every college rink he entered. Only 18 years old, he put up 71 points, the highest total by a freshman player since 1991–92. Eichel also won the Hobey Baker Memorial Award as the most outstanding player in the country that season. Paul Kariya, the University of Maine star who had 100 points in 1991–92, had been the only freshman to do so. It had been so long since Kariya's magnificent season that fans could hardly believe what they were seeing from the BU freshman.

And if he were going to be drafted any other season, he probably would have been the first overall pick in the draft. It just so happened that he shared a draft year with McDavid, who had an even more impressive season in the Ontario Hockey League (OHL). Thus, Eichel went No. 2 to the Buffalo Sabres, where he instantly became a fan favorite.

The Sabres were coming off of the worst records in the NHL the year before, and they needed a dose of hope. A sold-out crowd showed up for the season opener against the Ottawa Senators. Eichel was able to get the fans out of their seats. With the Sabres trailing 2–0 in the third period, Eichel popped into open space on the left side of the net and took a nice pass from teammate Marcus Foligno. Eichel then waited out Senators goalie Craig Anderson before firing a shot into the far corner. Goal!

Fans in Buffalo were looking for anything positive to hang on to after such a tough season the year before. Eichel's goal provided just that. Unfortunately

A COACH AND ROLE MODEL

Eichel is hardly the first young American star to enter the NHL with huge expectations. In fact, Sabres coach Phil Housley was once in the same position. The Sabres drafted Housley sixth overall in 1982. Like Eichel, he was immediately thrust into the Sabres' lineup at a young age. Housley excelled over eight seasons with the Sabres at the start of a 21-year career that landed him in the Hockey Hall of Fame. His connection to the team was one of the reasons he was hired in 2017 to help guide the rebuilding Sabres. Working with Eichel was a big attraction to the job for Housley as well. "He's a terrific talent," Housley said when he was hired. "I want to get the most out of him."

Eichel's NHL debut was a memorable one when the Sabres rookie scored his first career goal in the season opener.

for Eichel and the Sabres, there was still a lot more work to be done for the whole team. Buffalo continued to struggle, but at least now they had a player they could build around.

On the ice, Eichel stands out for just how effortless he makes everything look. He has a long, easy stride. Because of this, he doesn't look terribly fast. That is, until you see him blowing past a defenseman while barely breaking a sweat. He also seems to see the game several steps ahead of everyone else. Even more than that is that Eichel has that inner drive that can take a good player to the next level.

> **"HE'S ALWAYS LOOKING AT OTHER PLAYERS, OTHER GAMES."**
>
> —SABRES TEAMMATE JAKE MCCABE

"He's always looking at other players, other games," Sabres teammate Jake McCabe explained to USA *Hockey Magazine*. "He's one of those guys who really keeps track of how other guys are doing and he really wants to be the best. It's one of those things that drives him every day, and his bottom line is he just wants to win. Everything he does, I can't say enough, he really wants to win."

Wins were harder to come by in Buffalo than at BU, but the team's struggles provided an opportunity.

When the times are tough, great players find a way to raise their game. That's what Eichel did. He was the Sabres' leading scorer in two of his first three seasons, sometimes battling through injury and a weaker supporting cast.

> "WE HAVE TO COMMUNICATE A MESSAGE TO OUR FANS, OUR ORGANIZATION, OUR CITY THAT AS BAD AS THINGS WERE, WE'RE GOING TO CHANGE IT, WE'RE GOING TO CHANGE THINGS AROUND HERE."
>
> –JACK EICHEL

At the end of another tough season in 2017–18, Eichel started to show more of the leadership qualities the team had hoped would materialize as he matured. Players handle adversity in a lot of different ways, but Eichel decided to take the negative of a bad season for the team to motivate him and his teammates to make a change.

"We have to communicate a message to our fans, our organization, our city that as bad as things were, we're going to change it, we're going to change things around here," Eichel said after the disappointing

2017–18 season ended. "It starts with the guys in the room. It starts with me. It starts with the guys that are our leaders."

Eichel was already the star of the Sabres at that point, but it was at that moment, when the franchise was at one of its lower points, that Buffalo officially became Eichel's team and his city. When the brighter days come for the organization, it will probably be Eichel leading the team's young core to the next level.

JACK EICHEL AT-A-GLANCE

BIRTHPLACE: North Chelmsford, Massachusetts
BIRTH DATE: October 28, 1996
POSITION: Center
SHOOTS: Right
SIZE: 6'2", 206 pounds
TEAM: Buffalo Sabres
PREVIOUS TEAM: Boston University (NCAA) (2014–15)
DRAFTED BY THE SABRES SECOND OVERALL IN 2015

CHAPTER 4

JOHNNY GAUDREAU

All of his life, Johnny Gaudreau heard the same thing over and over: "You're too small to make it in hockey." Anyone who uttered those words to the admittedly undersized Gaudreau offered him just another person to prove wrong.

When Gaudreau was a young teenager, he started trying out for local teams that would play against other elite teams in various festivals. He made the team as a 13-year-old, but the next two years he was cut—often because he was one of the smallest players on the ice.

"I took not being included on those teams pretty hard," Gaudreau wrote in a *Players' Tribune* piece. "I'd looked up to smaller guys when I was younger. I'd watch (smaller) players like Danny Briere and Martin St. Louis, and quietly think to myself, 'Why not me?'

Johnny Gaudreau quickly showed why NHL scouts shouldn't underestimate shorter players.

"It was my dad who really lifted me up when I lost hope. He refused to let me believe that I wasn't good enough. 'They don't like you because you're small, John. That's it.' He'd always plant that seed in the back of my mind that I was going to prove everybody wrong. I was going to force people to ignore my size because of my production."

Even as Gaudreau got an opportunity to play in the USHL, the top junior circuit in the country, others continued to have their doubts. As a 17-year-old, he was the league's fourth leading scorer, rookie of the year, and the playoff MVP after leading the Dubuque Fighting Saints to the league's championship.

Despite his incredible season, the NHL's Central Scouting Bureau wasn't convinced. The bureau, which provides a public ranking prior to each NHL draft, listed Gaudreau as the 193rd best prospect in North America. Most players in that range would not expect to hear their names called in the draft.

At that time, Gaudreau was measured at 5 feet, 6 inches and 137 pounds. It was clear his size was still a concern. But it wasn't a concern for everyone. The Calgary Flames liked Gaudreau enough to take a chance on him in the fourth round of the 2011 NHL

Entry Draft. Some snickered that it was too early. Others thought he shouldn't have been drafted at all. But the Flames had been doing their homework on this undersized wonder.

"There are very few guys that I could tell you exactly where the first time I saw them, but he stood out," Calgary Flames scout Tod Button said. "I think he stood out because the goals were so high-end and because he was so small. That was his storyline, right? I was just laughing. I was thinking, 'Who is this little guy?'"

That little guy turned out to be one of the best players to come out of that 2011 draft despite being the 104th selection.

Still, the NHL would have to wait. Gaudreau's excellent USHL season earned him a scholarship to Boston College, one of the top hockey programs in the country. He got off to a slow start his freshman year, but about halfway through he started scoring in bunches. Just as he did as a USHL rookie, he played a starring role for Boston College as the Eagles won the national championship. Gaudreau scored a highlight-reel quality goal to give the Eagles the extra cushion it needed to beat Ferris State in the final. Now a national

Gaudreau's highlight-reel goal in the 2012 NCAA title game helped lead Boston College to the national championship.

TV audience got to see that little guy Button had grown so fond of.

Gaudreau spent two more years at Boston College. He won a World Junior Championship gold medal with Team USA during his sophomore season. As a junior, he won the Hobey Baker Memorial Award as college hockey's best player. He earned the nickname "Johnny Hockey," and people started to finally believe that maybe this kid could make something of himself in hockey.

Phil Housley is a longtime NHL defenseman and member of the Hockey Hall of Fame. He was Gaudreau's coach at the World Junior Championship, where the small winger led Team USA with seven goals. It didn't take Housley long to notice that Gaudreau was different.

"When I first met him I was pretty shocked," Housley recalled. "He looks like your little brother. (Then) he got on the ice and right away you could see that he plays the game in a way very few people do."

What Housley saw and what the world can now see on a daily basis in the NHL is that Gaudreau's size doesn't matter because opposing players can't seem to catch him. He's both fast and one of the best puck handlers in the NHL, making him very difficult to defend or even try to body check. It turns out that Gaudreau's size made it a necessity for him to focus on developing his skating and skills to make sure that he could keep progressing, but also to make sure he didn't get hurt.

"Keep your head up. Always," Gaudreau wrote in *The Player's Tribune* as his advice for smaller players like him. "You're not built to take heavy shots, so you have to be twice as careful out there."

It is pretty rare to see "Johnny Hockey" take a hard hit. He's usually making the guys that do try to hit him look pretty silly with some of his incredible stickhandling skills.

The Flames signed Gaudreau after his junior season at Boston College, just in time for Gaudreau to play in their last game of the season. He scored a goal on the only shot he took in the game.

THANK YOU, SKITTLES

Growing up in New Jersey, Johnny's father, Guy, owned the local ice arena. There were two sheets of ice and it allowed Johnny and younger brother Matthew a chance to skate pretty much whenever they wanted. But Johnny didn't really love the ice at first. So his father devised a plan to help him learn how to skate: Skittles. Guy would throw Skittles on the ice and have little Johnny skate to his favorite candy. Once Johnny would get to one Skittle and eat it, Guy would throw out another one. It worked.

The next year, his first full season in the NHL, he was a finalist for the Calder Memorial Trophy, the league's rookie of the year award. He made the NHL All-Star Game in each of his first four seasons, and in 2016 he was selected to play for Team North America, the 23-and-under super team, in the World Cup of Hockey. In 2016–17, he also won the Lady Byng Memorial Trophy as the NHL's most gentlemanly player after taking only two penalties the entire season. His trophy cabinet should only continue to fill up.

No one is saying he's too small anymore.

JOHNNY GAUDREAU AT-A-GLANCE

BIRTHPLACE: Salem, New Jersey
BIRTH DATE: August 13, 1993
POSITION: Left Wing
SHOOTS: Left
SIZE: 5'9", 157 pounds
TEAM: Calgary Flames
PREVIOUS TEAM: Boston College (NCAA) (2011–14)
DRAFTED BY THE FLAMES 104TH OVERALL IN 2011

CHAPTER 5

JAKE GUENTZEL

Jake Guentzel walked into a dream scenario when he was first called up to the NHL. It was November 2016, and Guentzel had been on fire for the Pittsburgh Penguins' minor league team. As injuries mounted for the Pens, a spot opened up on the NHL squad. So they called up the 22-year-old winger to fill the hole.

When Guentzel entered the team's dressing room for the first time, he looked around. He saw Sidney Crosby, arguably the best player in the game. He saw Evgeni Malkin, one of the league's most dangerous centers. He also saw veterans such as Kris Letang, Marc-Andre Fleury, and Phil Kessel. And these were not just star players; they were star players coming off a Stanley Cup title in 2016. And now Guentzel was one of them in just his second full pro season. He

Jake Guentzel has been one of the Pittsburgh Penguins' top scorers since debuting in 2016.

had little time to gawk, though. The team expected Guentzel to perform.

As nervous as Guentzel was to be among these superstar players, they made him feel at ease right away. Guentzel recalled Crosby saying to him, "Hey, you're here now, might as well have fun with it, eh?"

Though Guentzel says he was nervous, he sure didn't look it on his first shift. After the Penguins forced a turnover, Kessel hit a hard-charging Guentzel in stride. The rookie took the puck down the left side

MINNESOTA'S STICK BOY

Growing up the son of a hockey coach can have its advantages. When Guentzel was younger, his dad, Mike, was an assistant for the University of Minnesota men's hockey team. That meant that young Jake could be a stick boy for the team. At that time, Phil Kessel was the star freshman for the Golden Gophers. Little did either Kessel or Guentzel know that they would one day be teammates in the NHL, and not only that, they'd win a Stanley Cup together. When Jake got his first call-up to the Penguins, Kessel was one of the first teammates to greet him. "Hey kid, we're back together again, huh?" That night, Guentzel played on the same line with the guy he used to be a stick boy for.

and feathered a shot through New York Rangers goalie Antti Raanta's legs and in. His first shot in his first shift in the first minute of his first NHL game was a goal.

Afterward, the Penguins' broadcast cameras found Jake's family, who had flown in at the last minute to see his debut. No one in the building, not even Jake himself, was as excited about that goal as his older brother Ryan.

It got better, though, because before the first period was over, Guentzel scored again, this time on a rebound off of a Malkin chance. Not a bad first period in the NHL.

Guentzel ended up spending half of the 2016–17 season with the Penguins, appearing in 40 total games. He scored 16 goals in the regular season, but the youngster really cemented his rising star status in the playoffs.

During the playoff run, Guentzel was paired on the same line as Crosby. Some say anyone can play with the best player in the league and succeed, but Crosby has gone through a lot of other linemates over the years who couldn't hang with him. Guentzel was not only able to hang with Crosby; he thrived alongside the Penguins' captain.

"I think he's quietly competitive, but he's shown a lot of poise too," Crosby explained. "You see the situations he's been throw into, for a young player, that isn't always easy, but he's handled it well."

At 22 years old, under all the pressure that comes with playing in the playoffs, Guentzel was able to make a smooth transition to playing alongside the game's best center. Most credit Guentzel's hockey sense for that. That may have roots in his family. Father Mike Guentzel had been a coach at high levels of hockey, including American junior and college hockey. Older brothers Ryan and Gabe both played in college.

"He's picked up stuff off everybody he's ever played with," Mike Guentzel said. "How's a guy tying the skates? How's he working on his sticks? What color tape is he using? What time's he getting his uniform on before the pregame warm up? The mind's always working."

Over the years Jake developed a keen understanding of positioning on the ice. Part of that is out of necessity. At 5 feet 11 inches, he is often one of the smaller players on the ice. So he needs to both protect himself and find space to use his skills and make plays.

To reach the highest levels, though, Guentzel also needed the physical tools. The smartest player on the ice can't do much if he can't execute—even if he's playing on a line with Crosby. Needless to say, Guentzel can do that. He showed that as he helped power the Penguins to a second straight Stanley Cup win during that 2017 run.

En route to that championship, Guentzel scored 13 goals to lead all players in the postseason. He was one goal away from tying the record for most goals in a single playoff season by a rookie. He might not have gotten the record, but he did get his name on the Stanley Cup, which is probably better anyway.

JAKE GUENTZEL AT-A-GLANCE

BIRTHPLACE: Omaha, Nebraska

BIRTH DATE: October 6, 1994

POSITION: Center/Right Wing/Left Wing

SHOOTS: Left

SIZE: 5'11", 180 pounds

TEAM: Pittsburgh Penguins

PREVIOUS TEAM: University of Nebraska Omaha (NCAA) (2013–16)

DRAFTED BY THE PENGUINS 77TH OVERALL IN 2013

CHAPTER 6

CONNOR HELLEBUYCK

When Connor Hellebuyck was playing high school hockey in Michigan, he couldn't seem to get any scouts to look at him. The top-tier USHL passed on him. So did all of the teams in the second-tier North American Hockey League (NAHL). When that happens, a player's hopes of getting picked in the NHL draft are pretty slim, too. But then opportunity knocked for the teenage netminder. Though they had passed on him in the league's draft, the NAHL's Odessa Jackalopes invited Hellebuyck to a tryout.

"He's one of the best stories you could ever come up with," former Odessa general manager and goalie coach Joe Clark said. "Connor was on no one's radar. He was as much of an unknown as you can get. No one ever heard of him. No one had ever really seen him."

Connor Hellebuyck's long journey through juniors led him to the Winnipeg Jets.

Hellebuyck was one of eight goalies invited to try out for the team in west Texas. Because he hadn't been scouted much, the Odessa staff didn't know what to make of him. But after the tryout, Clark said Hellebuyck was a no-brainer to put on the team. So he spent a season nearly 1,500 miles away from his hometown of Commerce Township, Michigan.

"HE'S ONE OF THE BEST STORIES YOU COULD EVER COME UP WITH."

–ODESSA JACKALOPES GENERAL MANAGER JOE CLARK

Hellebuyck was a big kid, but he hadn't had a lot of formal goalie training. He just kept working and just kept getting better. He ended up playing 53 games for Odessa and recorded a .930 save percentage. That was enough to earn him honors as the NAHL's goalie and rookie of the year. Suddenly the college recruiters and scouts who didn't give him much of a thought while he was playing for Walled Lake Northern High School back in Michigan were intrigued by the big, athletic goaltender.

First came a scholarship offer from the University of Massachusetts-Lowell. Next came the bigger shock.

A year after going completely undrafted by any junior team, Hellebuyck heard his name called in the NHL draft. The Winnipeg Jets made him a fifth-round draft pick, 130th overall.

Most teams draft a player in the fifth round believing he can become a productive player. Within a year, the Jets knew they had a high-end goalie prospect on their hands. Hellebuyck became a dominant college goaltender. He was named the Hockey East Goalie of the Year as a freshman after putting up a .948 save percentage. That was one of the best save percentages in the history of college hockey. The following year he won the Mike Richter Award as college hockey's top goaltender. And soon after that sophomore season, he had an NHL contract in hand.

Hellebuyck spent a year with Winnipeg's minor league team, and he played so well in the American Hockey League (AHL) that Team USA asked him to come play for them in the World Championships. He ended up putting up the best numbers of any goalie in the tournament at only 21 years old, backstopping the Americans to the bronze medal. If there were any doubts left about his ability, his performance at that tournament crushed them.

Hellebuyck backstopped the Jets to the 2018 Western Conference Final before falling to the Vegas Golden Knights.

It hasn't been all smooth sailing for Hellebuyck at the NHL level. He had a nice start in 2015–16, but the 2016–17 season was a bit forgettable as Hellebuyck didn't perform up to the high standards he had set for himself during the previous few years.

No stranger to hard work and proving people wrong, Hellebuyck committed himself to not letting another season like that happen. So he worked hard in the summer before the 2017–18 season. It seemed that all of the work paid off because from the second the season started, Hellebuyck brought his "A" game. His coaches and teammates noticed right away that he was looking different between the pipes than he did the season before.

"He looked stronger in the net," Jets coach Paul Maurice said early in the 2017–18 season. "(He was) able to hold his body position quite a bit longer; not nearly as much movement in his game."

Power and strength have always been key components of Hellebuyck's game, but there also has to be some mental control and focus to make sure a goalie isn't making things too hard on himself and

EYES ON THE PRIZE

Goalies are known for being a bit quirky, and like many of his peers, Hellebuyck goes through some unique routines before every game. One of the zanier ones is if there is a camera in the Jets' dressing room, he makes a point to stare directly into the lens and not break eye contact until the camera operator moves on to another subject or leaves. This routine went viral on social media during the 2018 Stanley Cup Playoffs. Hellebuyck stared right into the recording camera while he got his pads on before the game. Suddenly Hellebuyck was staring straight into the living rooms of NBCSN's television audience for several seconds, almost to the point where it became unsettling.

getting too tired. A goalie also has to have confidence in his ability to make the big saves. Getting all of those things to work together can be the hard part, but Hellebuyck apparently found the right mix.

"My game is mainly mental," Hellebuyck told the *Winnipeg Free Press.* "I think it's getting my confidence, and not only my confidence but the feel of the game right. If I'm comfortable in the net, I'm gonna do things I don't realize I'm doing. Once I found that, I implemented the right things into my game."

He must have implemented the right things into his game because he was one of the league's best goalies in 2017–18. Hellebuyck led the NHL with 44 wins in 67 appearances and also had a .924 save

> "MY GAME IS MAINLY MENTAL. I THINK IT'S GETTING MY CONFIDENCE, AND NOT ONLY MY CONFIDENCE BUT THE FEEL OF THE GAME RIGHT. IF I'M COMFORTABLE IN THE NET, I'M GONNA DO THINGS I DON'T REALIZE I'M DOING. ONCE I FOUND THAT, I IMPLEMENTED THE RIGHT THINGS INTO MY GAME."
>
> —CONNOR HELLEBUYCK

percentage. He finished second in the voting for the Vezina Trophy given to the league's best goaltender. He even picked up votes for the Hart Trophy, which goes to the league's MVP.

To go from undrafted by any junior team to one of the best goalies in the NHL in about six years is one of the more incredible feats a young player has made in the NHL in some time.

CONNOR HELLEBUYCK
AT-A-GLANCE

BIRTHPLACE: Commerce, Michigan
BIRTH DATE: May 19, 1993
POSITION: Goaltender
CATCHES: Left
SIZE: 6'4", 207 pounds
TEAM: Winnipeg Jets
PREVIOUS TEAM: University of Massachusetts-Lowell (NCAA) (2012–14)
DRAFTED BY THE JETS 130TH OVERALL IN 2012

CHAPTER 7

SETH JONES

With dad Popeye Jones playing in the National Basketball Association (NBA), it wasn't a stretch to think Seth Jones was going to become a great athlete. Popeye just never expected his son's sport to be hockey.

Thanks to Popeye's basketball career, however, Seth found himself in the right place at just the right time. In 1999, Popeye was traded to the Denver Nuggets. That happened to be right when the local hockey team, the Colorado Avalanche, was in the midst of a golden generation. Like many kids in the Denver area, Seth and his brothers, Justin and Caleb, fell for hockey . . . hard.

The Nuggets and Avalanche shared the same building. Not knowing much about the sport himself,

The son of a basketball star, Seth Jones now patrols the blue line for the Columbus Blue Jackets.

Popeye took full advantage of the situation. He found Avalanche captain Joe Sakic one day and asked him for some advice.

"I said that my kids are interested in playing hockey and I have no clue what to do," Popeye Jones recalled. "He looked and saw how tall I was. He said, 'By the looks of you, they are going to be very tall. Make sure they know how to skate.' I told my boys, 'Joe Sakic said you better know how to skate. You have to be a great skater.'"

So the Jones brothers started taking skating lessons before they ever picked up a hockey stick. That helped provide the foundation for Seth to become one of the best young defenders in the game. At 6-foot-4 and 210 pounds, he didn't grow quite as tall as his dad, who played at 6-foot-8 and 250 pounds. Yet Seth skates as smoothly as any big defender in the NHL today.

In 2007, the family moved back to Texas, where Seth had been born. Hockey had been growing in popularity there. Despite the lack of natural ice in Texas, the state now had good youth programs. Soon, Seth became one of the very best players in his age-group and started generating a lot of hype.

Jones was an interesting story. Not many sons of NBA players pick hockey as their passion. Not only that, but to come from a non-traditional hockey state such as Texas, Jones was not your average hockey player. And in 2013, the Nashville Predators selected Jones fourth overall in the NHL Entry Draft. That made him the first black player to be a top-five pick. Jones's background gave him a lot of visibility. It made Jones an inspiration to a lot of kids. Young non-white players saw that a black star could thrive in the predominantly white sport.

"There have been a few African-American kids who have come up to me and said, 'You're my favorite player," Jones said. "They have my jersey or my T-shirt jersey on. That's pretty cool. I am for whatever I can do to grow the game in all aspects. A black kid cheering for hockey or cheering for me is pretty rare. When you see that, you get pretty excited."

> **"THERE HAVE BEEN A FEW AFRICAN-AMERICAN KIDS WHO HAVE COME UP TO ME AND SAID, 'YOU'RE MY FAVORITE PLAYER.'"**
>
> **–SETH JONES**

Jones thrived with the Predators as a rookie in 2013–14. Despite being only 19, he even got consideration to play for Team USA at the Olympics. Three years into his career, however, Jones got a rather big surprise. Nashville traded him to the Columbus Blue Jackets for star forward Ryan Johansen.

It's rare to see two young stars traded for each other like that, but it ended up working out well for both players. Jones is pretty much the total package as a defenseman. He skates well, plus he has good moves and a hard shot. What really stands out, though, is how smart he is. Jones is the kind of defensemen coaches never have to worry about because he makes very few mistakes and makes a lot of good decisions when he has the puck on his stick.

This helped Jones thrive immediately when he joined Columbus, and he soon became the team's No. 1 defenseman. Prior to his first full season with the Blue Jackets, in 2016–17, Jones was selected for Team North America, the U23 squad that competed against top national teams in the 2016 World Cup of Hockey. The progression continued into the NHL season, as Jones was named to the 2017 NHL All-Star Game. One year later, he finished fourth in voting for the Norris

With a strong all-around game, Jones has become the No. 1 defenseman in Columbus.

Trophy as the league's top defenseman. His stock has only continued to rise.

Thomas Vanek, who at the time had already played more than 900 games in the NHL, offered this assessment of Jones during the 2017–18 season: "Jonesy is by far the best defenseman I've ever played with."

Vanek probably wasn't too biased with that statement either. He played only 19 games with the Blue Jackets that year, but he had been around the league more than a decade. So that's pretty high praise from a guy who has seen his share of defensemen over stints on several teams across the NHL.

AMERICAN PIPELINE

During the mid-1990s, American hockey was falling behind the rest of the world. USA Hockey responded by creating the National Team Development Program (NTDP). Beginning in 1997–98, top 17- and 18-year-old players from around the country moved to Michigan. There, they received elite training while playing against older opponents all while attending high school. The NTDP was a success, especially for players from non-traditional hockey states like Seth Jones. In addition to Jones, other US players who played with the NTDP include Jack Eichel, Patrick Kane, Phil Kessel, Auston Matthews, and Ryan Suter.

It all comes back to that foundation that Jones built in those skating lessons that were suggested by no less an authority than Joe Sakic. Everything starts with the skating and Jones's advanced hockey intelligence. That's a big reason why many believe the best is yet to come for Jones, who has been a role model for young hockey players in so many ways already.

According to Popeye, Seth was actually a pretty good basketball player, too, but the ice called to him in a way the hard court didn't. The hockey world sure is glad for that, as now we all get to watch Jones continue to excel at the game's highest level.

SETH JONES AT-A-GLANCE

BIRTHPLACE: Arlington, Texas
BIRTH DATE: October 3, 1994
POSITION: Defense
SHOOTS: Right
SIZE: 6'4", 210 pounds
TEAM: Columbus Blue Jackets
PREVIOUS TEAM(S): Nashville Predators (NHL) (2013–16), Portland Winterhawks (Western Hockey League) (2012–13)
DRAFTED BY THE PREDATORS FOURTH OVERALL IN 2013

CHAPTER 8

PATRIK LAINE

Watch Patrik Laine for just a few minutes and two things will become apparent right away. The first is obvious: at 6 feet, 5 inches and more than 200 pounds, he's a pretty big guy. The second is that the Tampere, Finland, native shoots the puck about as well as anyone playing in the NHL today.

It took only a few weeks into his rookie season for Laine to show how special his shot was. In an early-season game during that 2016–17 season, Laine and his Winnipeg Jets were playing Auston Matthews and the Toronto Maple Leafs. The previous June, Laine, a right winger, was drafted second. Matthews, a center, had gone first. The media started to play up a rivalry between the two forwards, making that late-October meeting a game with a lot of eyeballs on it.

Patrik Laine has proven himself to be a top-level scorer with the Winnipeg Jets.

Matthews and the Leafs took some of the drama out of it by building a 4–0 lead. But that just gave the Jets reason to unleash their not-so-secret weapon, and Laine went off.

The young Finn scored two goals in regulation, the first on a nifty turnaround shot that the goalie never saw coming. The second goal tied the game 4–4 with less than a minute to play in regulation. Laine took a pass and, without stopping the puck, rifled a shot into the wide-open net. The MTS Centre exploded with cheers as the Jets came all the way back from a deficit that looked too difficult to make up.

As loud as the crowd got for the game-tying goal off of Laine's stick, the biggest crowd pop was to come in overtime. Matthews had a golden opportunity to end the game for the Maple Leafs as he broke in all alone on Jets goalie Michael Hutchinson. The Winnipeg netminder made a save, and the puck went right to Jets defenseman Dustin Byfuglien. He sent a long pass to Laine streaking down the right side. It was a 2-on-1, but Laine had eyes only for the net. He wired a wrist shot past Toronto goalie Frederik Andersen to give the Jets an improbable 5–4 win.

After the game, Laine got quite the shout-out. Hockey Hall of Famer Teemu Selanne tweeted, "New sheriff in town . . . Congrats Patrik Laine . . . wow . . . "

In addition to being one of the greatest Finnish goal scorers in the history of the game, Selanne had also starred for the original Jets, who had moved to Arizona in 1996. When Selanne was a rookie with the Jets, he scored an NHL rookie record 76 goals. So that was pretty high praise coming from him.

Laine continued to rule the ice, finishing his rookie season with 36 goals. He was just behind Matthews for the Calder Memorial Trophy as rookie of the year.

HE'S A GAMER

Laine might shoot a puck and score goals as well as anyone who has picked up a hockey stick, but his favorite hobby is probably not all that different from yours: playing video games. Laine says he probably plays too much, but it's been a good way for him to stay in touch with his friends in Finland and friends on other NHL teams. Laine says his off-day schedule includes waking up, going to practice, working out, going home, and turning on his PlayStation. Laine's favorite game is *Call of Duty*.

Within that first year, Laine had already staked his claim to being one of the NHL's top goal scorers.

The following year Laine was chasing his idol, Washington Capitals superstar Alex Ovechkin, for the Rocket Richard Trophy, which goes to the top goal scorer in the league. Laine finished second, but he had won the respect of Ovechkin during the chase.

"He's a great talent and still young and still can produce a lot of dangers for different teams," Ovechkin said. "Obviously, his shot is pretty amazing."

Laine had grown up with an Ovechkin poster in his room and tried to pattern his game after the Capitals captain.

"He's been my biggest idol when I was growing up, so it's pretty unreal to hear something like that, him talking about me," Laine said.

There are a lot of factors that make Laine's shot so dangerous, as Ovechkin noted. The first is how quickly he is able to get the puck off his stick. A player's release on his shot is possibly more important than the power he puts behind it. The quicker the puck gets off the stick, the harder it is for the goalie to track it. Laine is able to produce both a quick release and a lot of power on his shots, which is a really troubling combo for goaltenders.

By his second NHL season, Laine was already one of the league's top goal-scorers.

"Any time he shoots the puck, not just in tight, but even if it's from the outside, he's got a good release, but he's got such soft hands for a big guy," former Jets teammate Paul Stastny said. "It always surprises the goalie, and it seems like when he does shoot it, there's a scoring chance or there's a rebound."

When you have a player like that, it forces other teams to prepare for games differently. They can't focus on only winning the game; they have to find a way to shut down such a great scorer. Winnipeg captain Blake Wheeler believes that Laine had already gotten that level of respect and concern from other teams by his second season in the league. It gave the Jets a competitive advantage.

> **"THIS IS THE THING I WANT TO DO THE REST OF MY LIFE. I LOVE PLAYING HOCKEY. I LOVE EVERYTHING ABOUT IT, SO IT'S JUST AWESOME TO BE HERE EVERY DAY."**
>
> **–PATRIK LAINE**

"He changes a lot of what we're able to do," Wheeler said. "It's a lot like when you play against Ovechkin: you just have to be aware of where he is, especially on the power play, so it opens up so much ice for everyone else, having that threat out there. He's a special talent."

Perhaps the most important aspect of Laine's scoring ability is that it comes from his passion for the game. Everyone loves to score goals, but the best goal scorers love it more than anyone else.

"This is the thing I want to do the rest of my life," Laine said. "I love playing hockey. I love everything about it, so it's just awesome to be here every day."

There have been many great Finnish players to enter the NHL, with Selanne probably being the best. But there's a good chance that when Laine's career is over, he's going to go down as not only one of the best Finnish goal scorers the game has seen, but one of the best of any nationality. After already having Selanne in the early 1990s, the fans in Winnipeg are getting spoiled once again with Laine.

PATRIK LAINE AT-A-GLANCE

BIRTHPLACE: Tampere, Finland
BIRTH DATE: April 19, 1998
POSITION: Right Wing
SHOOTS: Right
SIZE: 6'5", 206 pounds
TEAM: Winnipeg Jets
PREVIOUS TEAM: Tappara (SM-Liiga) (2014–16)
DRAFTED BY THE JETS SECOND OVERALL IN 2016

CHAPTER 9

NATHAN MacKINNON

Cole Harbour, a town on the eastern coast of Nova Scotia, Canada, has a population of about 25,000 people. Amazingly, this small town has produced two No. 1 overall NHL draft picks. Sidney Crosby was first. Drafted in 2005, he went on to become the best player of his generation for the Pittsburgh Penguins. The second was Nathan MacKinnon. Drafted first overall by the Colorado Avalanche in 2013, his path to the NHL was awfully similar to Crosby's.

Coming up eight years behind Crosby, MacKinnon wanted to be just like the Penguins' captain. Posters and other Crosby memorabilia covered MacKinnon's childhood room. Both were centers. And soon enough, the young star was following in "Sid the Kid's" footsteps.

From Nova Scotia to Colorado, Nathan MacKinnon has thrived at all levels of the sport.

Just as Crosby had done, MacKinnon made the decision to head to the United States to play his age 14 and 15 seasons at the famed Shattuck-St. Mary's prep school in Faribault, Minnesota. After his second year at Shattuck, MacKinnon moved on to junior hockey. He was the No. 1 pick in the Quebec Major Junior Hockey

SHATTUCK-ST. MARY'S HOCKEY FACTORY

It's known in the hockey world simply as "Shattuck." Everyone knows what that means. Tucked away in Faribault, a town in southern Minnesota, Shattuck-St. Mary's School has become one of the premier prep schools in the world for aspiring hockey players. Students have come from all over, but none more famous than Sidney Crosby. MacKinnon is right up there in famous alumni as well. But there have been many more NHL players who skated at the vaunted hockey school. Among them: Jonathan Toews, Zach Parise, Jack Johnson, Drew Stafford, Kyle Okposo, Jonathan Toews, Derek Stepan, and Patrick Eaves. On the women's side, the school has produced US Olympic gold medalists Amanda Kessel, Jocelyne and Monique Lamoureux, Alyssa Gagliardi, and Brianna Decker. So yeah, they're pretty good at hockey out there.

League (QMJHL) draft, again just like Crosby. After two years playing in the QMJHL in his home province with the Halifax Mooseheads, it was already apparent that MacKinnon was on his way to stardom.

To complete the Crosby comparisons, the Avalanche made MacKinnon the No. 1 draft pick in 2013. But in 2013–14, MacKinnon did something Crosby did not. MacKinnon finished that season as the NHL's rookie of the year, winning the Calder Memorial Trophy after leading all rookies in scoring that season.

Another way that MacKinnon is different from Crosby, and one of the reasons he is such an effective player, is that he is one of the NHL's most explosive skaters. He credits his 5 a.m. power skating lessons before school while growing up in Cole Harbour for helping him become a great skater.

"It's always been a strength of mine since I was a little kid. I think I kind of picked it up more naturally than others but I did work really hard at it," MacKinnon said in 2017.

"My dad, thankfully, took me to power skating before school. A lot of kids didn't like doing that—and I didn't even like doing it that much—but my dad kept encouraging me and I'm glad I kept with it."

With MacKinnon's speed, opposing players have the tough task of keeping up with the Avalanche forward.

In 2014, MacKinnon's speed was put to the test in a pretty unique way. Equipment maker CCM had MacKinnon skate head-to-head against Canadian short-track speed skating gold medalist Charles Hamelin in a race between the blue lines on a hockey rink. Both started from a standstill, but MacKinnon was in his full hockey gear while Hamlin was in the windsuit that speed skaters wear at the Olympics. Still, MacKinnon won the 50-foot race by a single stride, showing just how powerful and quick a skater he is.

MacKinnon works extremely hard at building leg strength, but skating can also be a bit of a mental game. Being a great skater requires a lot of focus and body control. You have to keep yourself in the best possible position to generate the power required to speed up and down the ice. It's also different to skate when you have the puck than it is without it.

"He's the fastest skater in the league with the puck," Avalanche teammate Gabriel Landeskog said. "It's easy to be fast without the puck, but when you

69

have the puck it's a completely different thing. That's what Nate does so well.

"That's what the best players do. They're a step ahead, and I think when it comes to Nate, when you're able to move at a high pace and stickhandle at the same time and make moves at the same time, that's when it's hard on defensemen."

The NHL continues to become a faster league, and MacKinnon remains a step ahead, with very few players in the league able to match him stride for stride. His ability to keep defenders on their heels and sometimes just blow right past them on the way to another highlight reel goal is a big reason MacKinnon has become one of the league's most exciting players.

Following MacKinnon's big rookie season, the Avalanche struggled a bit. The 2017–18 season proved to be MacKinnon's big breakout after. He had 97 points in only 74 games, improving on his previous season's point total by 44 points.

Jumps in production like that are pretty rare. MacKinnon ended up finishing second in Hart Trophy voting as the league's MVP, but more important, he reminded the NHL that he was just getting warmed up. Only 22 years old, he had played the leading role in getting the Avs back to the playoffs.

When visitors arrive in Cole Harbour, a sign welcomes them. "Welcome to Cole Harbour, Home of Sidney Crosby," it reads. It's only natural that Crosby would get top billing, seeing as he's won multiple Stanley Cups and Hart Trophies. If MacKinnon keeps up his strong play, though, the town might soon have to update its sign.

NATHAN MACKINNON
AT-A-GLANCE

BIRTHPLACE: Halifax, Nova Scotia

BIRTH DATE: September 1, 1995

POSITION: Center

SHOOTS: Right

SIZE: 6', 205 pounds

TEAM: Colorado Avalanche

PREVIOUS TEAM: Halifax Mooseheads (QMJHL) (2011–13)

DRAFTED BY THE AVALANCHE FIRST OVERALL IN 2013

CHAPTER 10

AUSTON MATTHEWS

The disappointment of another losing season quickly turned to excitement when the Toronto Maple Leafs earned the first overall pick in the 2016 NHL Entry Draft. Using that pick to select American center Auston Matthews only amped up the anticipation. And when the 19-year-old Matthews finally made his debut on October 12, 2016, he blew even the most optimistic expectations out of the water.

On the road against the Ottawa Senators, Matthews wasted little time showing just what he could do, netting his first goal only 8:21 into the first period. It doesn't get better than scoring your first goal in your first game, right? Well, Matthews was about to make it better.

Auston Matthews turned heads when he went from Phoenix to hockey-mad Toronto in 2016.

Later in the first period, the rookie caught a loose puck at the Senators' blue line. He stickhandled around two players, took the puck into the zone, got around Ottawa's superstar defenseman Erik Karlsson, took the puck to the net, and slid a shot right under Sens goalie Craig Anderson. It was one of the most impressive goals scored in the entire 2016–17 season. But Matthews *still* wasn't done. In the second period, Matthews added two more goals. That made him the first player in the history of the NHL to score four goals in his debut.

It was an incredible way to start a career that is sure to bring more accolades, but one of the things that makes Matthews' rise to the NHL all the more impressive is his non-traditional hockey background.

Matthews was born in California, and his family soon moved to Arizona. Known for its deserts and hot temperatures, Arizona wasn't exactly an ice hockey hotbed. That began to change in a big way in 1996. That's when the original Winnipeg Jets moved to Phoenix and became the Coyotes. Matthews was born one year later, in 1997.

Still, hockey wasn't exactly a big part of the Matthews family. Auston's father, Brian, had been a baseball player. His mother, Ema, came from Mexico, not knowing anything about hockey. So without the Coyotes, Auston might never have found the game.

Thankfully for hockey fans everywhere, he had the Coyotes. Attending a Coyotes game as a toddler sealed hockey as Matthews's first love. His parents made the necessary sacrifices to help pay for Auston's youth hockey. But raising a hockey player in Arizona was not all that easy, it turned out.

There weren't many ice arenas in and around Scottsdale, where Auston grew up. Luckily, though, there was a small arena called Ozzie Ice, only 10 minutes from the Matthews's home. The ice surface wasn't as big as the ones they play on in the NHL, and it couldn't hold organized games. That didn't stop Auston from spending many days honing his skills there, sometimes playing against kids who were much older than he was.

"You couldn't go anywhere on the ice where someone wasn't within 20 feet of you," Brian Matthews recalled. "You had to learn how to use your hands, how to think ahead, where the puck was going to go, who was coming, how to turn, how to get away from traffic, create space—all of that stuff—in such a small

Matthews's quick shot and adaptability make him a potential goal-scorer for the Maple Leafs on a nightly basis.

little window of ice. A lot of kids here developed a lot of really good skills there. They were forced to."

One benefit of playing on a smaller surface was that it forced Matthews to get his shot off very quickly. Still today, that's one of his best and most noticeable skills. Matthews has added many tweaks to his shot through the years, giving him one of the most unique shot releases in the game. It's something that opposing players often marvel at.

Even as Auston got bigger and better, he still came back to those unique skills that he honed on the smaller ice surface. Being able to stickhandle around oncoming defenders, fitting into tight spots with the puck, and making laser-fast decisions have all been big parts of Matthews's game.

Matthews certainly wasn't the first kid from Arizona who dreamed of playing in the NHL. Many of them had to leave the state, however, and go to a place such as Michigan or Canada, where hockey is more accessible and competitive. Matthews didn't leave, however. At least not until he was older. He stuck with the programs in Arizona up until his under-17 season. That's when USA Hockey invited him to play with other top teenagers at the NTDP in Ann Arbor, Michigan. He spent his last two seasons there before becoming a professional in 2015. So he is truly an Arizona-developed hockey player.

Make no mistake, though, Matthews's rise to the NHL is driven completely by him. Having the physical tools is one thing, but the desire to be great is what often separates the very good from the best.

"He's a smart guy and he understands what's going on," Maple Leafs coach Mike Babcock said during Matthews's second NHL season. "The other thing about him is he wants to be great, and if you want to be great, that's every day. It's not once in a while. It's

NOTHING BEATS MOM'S HOME COOKING

Most players go on to college or junior leagues after high school. Matthews wasn't one of them. Instead he played the 2015–16 season with the ZSC Lions in Zurich, Switzerland. (He became eligible for the draft after that season.) Auston and his mother Ema moved to Switzerland. They lived together, and she was able to cook for Auston, often making his favorite meals that have roots in her native Mexico. His favorite, according to Ema, was her chicken tortilla soup. Ema never thought she'd have a hockey player for a son. In fact, she never thought she'd leave Mexico before she met Brian Matthews. Now she's one of the more well-known hockey moms in the NHL. She is shown on TV at Maple Leafs games supporting her son, whom she lovingly calls "Papi."

every single day. He obviously picked that up early as a young man and brings that each and every day. He loves hockey, he loves people and he doesn't mind sharing himself."

Nothing has been common about Matthews's rise to NHL stardom or his skills. Who could have foreseen a kid from Scottsdale, Arizona, becoming the face of one of Canada's oldest and most prized hockey organizations? Thanks to the sacrifices his parents made to make sure he could keep playing and to his own work ethic and desire to become one of the very best players in the league, Matthews' NHL story is only just beginning.

AUSTON MATTHEWS AT-A-GLANCE

BIRTHPLACE: San Ramon, California
BIRTH DATE: September 17, 1997
POSITION: Center
SHOOTS: Left
SIZE: 6'3", 216 pounds
TEAM: Toronto Maple Leafs
PREVIOUS TEAM: ZSC Lions (Swiss National League A) (2015–16)
DRAFTED BY THE MAPLE LEAFS FIRST OVERALL IN 2016

CHAPTER 11

CHARLIE McAVOY

Most NHL teams are pretty cautious when they bring their prized young prospects into the league. After all, the NHL is the world's best hockey. Teams are wary of putting too much pressure on the young players. During the 2017 Stanley Cup Playoffs, however, the Boston Bruins did not have that luxury. They really needed a defenseman.

Only a few weeks prior, the Bruins had signed their 2016 first-round pick Charlie McAvoy to his first pro contract. It was an amateur tryout deal with their AHL team, the Providence Bruins. McAvoy had just finished his sophomore year at Boston University. The Bruins thought ending the season with Providence would give the young player a nice taste of pro hockey to close out the season.

By the time he arrived in Boston, Charlie McAvoy had a proven track record in big games.

The plan quickly went awry thanks to injuries at the big club. With the Bruins preparing to face the Ottawa Senators in the first round of the NHL playoffs, they suddenly needed a defenseman. McAvoy got the call.

It was a tough decision for team officials. McAvoy had played only four games in the AHL. His NHL experience was zero. But Bruins officials looked at the player's background. They saw he had played in some big games in college and with US youth national teams. Only a few months prior, McAvoy captained Team USA at the World Junior Championship. Playing in a tough environment in Montreal, he led the Americans to the gold medal against Canada. Then back at BU, McAvoy led his team back to the NCAA Tournament for the second year in a row.

> "CHARLIE IS A GUY UP TO THIS POINT WHO HAS HAD NO PROBLEM BEING IN THE LIMELIGHT, THE BIG GAME."
>
> –BRUINS COACH BRUCE CASSIDY

"Charlie is a guy up to this point who has had no problem being in the limelight, the big game," Bruins coach Bruce Cassidy said when the team called him up. "We'll hope that continues."

Now that McAvoy was in the NHL, most assumed he would be a depth defenseman. Maybe he'd play a few minutes a game to give some of the veterans a rest. After all, even though he had big-game experience, how was a 19-year-old kid supposed to come into one of the most intense postseasons in professional sports and have a lot of success?

There was no easing him in. McAvoy was put on the top defense pairing with Bruins captain Zdeno Chara. Chara is 20 years older than McAvoy. The young player couldn't have asked for a better defensive partner to start his career. Chara had won a Stanley Cup, was a seven-time league All-Star, and had won a Norris Trophy as the NHL's best defenseman. And if McAvoy was going to play with Chara, that meant he was going to be playing a lot.

The Bruins won the first game of the series with McAvoy playing more than 24 minutes in the game. That is a massive workload for even the most experienced NHL defensemen. In Game 5, McAvoy played for more than 31 minutes. That meant he was out there for more than half of the game.

Making his NHL debut in the 2017 playoffs, McAvoy quickly became a big part of the Bruins' defensive core.

Unfortunately, Game 5 was the only other game the Bruins won in that first-round matchup.

The Bruins knew they had a special player on their hands when they picked McAvoy in the draft. Now they believed they had a guy who could grow into a dominant force in the league. With Chara getting older, the team would soon need a replacement. This kid from Long Beach, New York, sure looked like he might fit the bill as the team's future No. 1 defenseman.

Having already played his first six games in the NHL, McAvoy was more than ready to start the 2017–18 season, his first official year in the NHL. Sure enough, the Bruins put him with Chara again. This made

GROWING UP A RIVAL

When McAvoy was growing up in Long Beach, New York, he idolized members of the New York Rangers. The one he liked most was Brian Leetch, who helped the Rangers win the Stanley Cup three years before McAvoy was born. "I used to watch those tapes of the '94 Stanley Cup run," McAvoy told the *New York Post* before he was drafted. "He was a guy who, as a defenseman, played the offensive side of the game better than anyone. And that was definitely a reason I play that kind of style. I wanted to play like him. He was my hero. The way he played was the way I wanted to play."

McAvoy a top-pairing defenseman at only 20 years old. He had a tremendous year, putting up 32 points despite missing 19 games with injuries. McAvoy also missed time after having to have a small procedure on his heart to fix a minor issue that the team had discovered the previous season. Despite all of that, McAvoy was able to come back and help the Bruins in the playoffs, once again playing major minutes.

"He's obviously a skilled player. Skates well, moves the puck well, sees the ice well," Chara said of his young defense partner. "What do I like best about him? That he's quickly able to adapt to our system and our game. We saw it in the playoffs (last season). He stepped in and gave us a contribution right away. He didn't seem to be nervous, or caught in a situation where he'd be distracted."

McAvoy learned a lot just from playing alongside Chara as well. Having a defenseman like that as an on-ice mentor is an advantage most young defensemen in the NHL couldn't dream of.

"The way (Chara) controls the game is just awesome," McAvoy said. "There aren't many people who can do it like that. When he gets the puck, it's (calming). He's so strong defensively. I know he's going to win his battles. Just being on the ice with him, you know it's going to be good."

In addition to the age gap, there's a pretty big size gap between Chara, who is 6-foot-9, and McAvoy, who is 6 feet. But McAvoy has proven that he is very strong for his age and isn't afraid to be physical. McAvoy delivered several big hits in his rookie season to let the league know that even if they try to stay away from Chara, they're going to have to deal with him.

Despite having a lot thrown at him very early in his career, McAvoy has met every challenge head-on and has exceeded expectations by rolling up his sleeves and going to work.

CHARLIE McAVOY AT-A-GLANCE

BIRTHPLACE: Long Beach, New York
BIRTH DATE: December 21, 1997
POSITION: Defense
SHOOTS: Right
SIZE: 6', 208 pounds
TEAM: Boston Bruins
PREVIOUS TEAM: Boston University (NCAA) (2015–17)
DRAFTED BY THE BRUINS 14TH OVERALL IN 2016

CHAPTER 12

CONNOR McDAVID

For much of Connor McDavid's life in hockey, he's been considered exceptional. Scouts could tell from a young age that McDavid offered the combination of speed, skill, and hockey intelligence that today's NHL game is built on. By the time he made his NHL debut with the Edmonton Oilers in 2015, those abilities had blossomed not just compared with his peers, but even against players much older than him.

McDavid had already won two scoring titles by the time he was 21 years old. During the first of those seasons, he also won the Hart Trophy as the league's MVP. At age 20, he was the third-youngest player to do so.

To anyone who saw McDavid playing as a youngster, none of this came as a surprise. Just like

Connor McDavid caught the eye of fans from a young age and lived up to the hype with the Oilers.

Wayne Gretzky and Sidney Crosby before him, McDavid was anointed hockey's next big thing long before his first NHL season.

The comparisons to Gretzky—the NHL's most dominant scorer of all time—began when McDavid was only 14. The teenager was already blowing away opponents with his incredible skating ability. In fact, he was so well thought of that the OHL allowed him to join at age 15. The OHL, a top junior league for players younger than 20, usually requires players to be at least 16 years old. And not only did the league let McDavid join early; the Erie Otters selected him with the first pick in the league's draft.

The decision paid off. McDavid was the OHL Rookie of the Year. He also joined players two years older than him on Canada's U18 national team. Again, he thrived. McDavid led the U18 World Championships in scoring and was named the tournament MVP. His Canada squad, meanwhile, won the gold medal. If hardcore hockey fans hadn't already heard of McDavid, they had now.

No player that young had ever dominated the tournament. For McDavid to take over at only 15 years old was eye-opening. It showed that he really was special and worthy of the exceptional hype. The only problem for NHL fans? They'd still need to wait two more years before he was eligible to be drafted.

During those next two years, McDavid helped the Otters go from one of the OHL's worst teams to one of its best in a single season. He also collected a lot more hardware. In 2014–15, McDavid also helped Canada win the World Junior Championship. At the end of the season, he was named the OHL's most outstanding player and the player of the year in all of Canadian junior hockey.

The comparisons to Gretzky and Crosby were now more relevant than ever. Even Gretzky agreed.

"He's as good as I've seen in the last 30 years, the best player to come into the league in the last 30 years, the best to come along since (Mario) Lemieux and (Sidney) Crosby," Gretzky said in the buildup to the 2015 NHL Entry Draft.

As it turned out, Gretzky's old team had the first pick in the draft. It was no surprise when they used it to pick McDavid.

Gretzky had been around for the Oilers' glory days, when they won five Stanley Cups from 1984 to 1990. Life after that hadn't been so successful. And after making the Stanley Cup Final in 2006, the Oilers began losing. A lot. By the time McDavid arrived they had a reputation for being one of the worst teams in the league. In fact, the team had actually picked first overall three other times in the previous five years before the 2015 draft. There was belief in Edmonton, however, that this time the team had gotten the pick right.

Just as Gretzky had done almost 30 years prior, McDavid injected a new level of optimism in the fan base. And just like Crosby and Gretzky, McDavid scored his first career goal in his third NHL game. It wasn't his prettiest goal, as he redirected a shot into

A COLLECTOR'S ITEM

Despite being in the NHL for only a few years, McDavid is already one of the league's most popular players among fans. In June 2018, one of his rookie cards was sold for a record $55,655. That made it the highest-priced modern era hockey trading card ever. It's pretty rare for someone to spend that much on any card, let alone one for a player who is only starting his career. If McDavid lives up to what everyone expects him to be, though, that price might look like a steal after he retires.

the net past Dallas Stars goalie Kari Lehtonen. But that opened the floodgates.

The young superstar showed the flashes of speed and skill that had made him famous in his junior hockey days. However, an injury interrupted his rookie season, knocking him out for three months. The missed time cost McDavid the rookie of the year trophy, but the stage was set for a very exciting second season.

Fully healthy, McDavid was able to dominate the league during the next two seasons. He topped 100 points both years and started staking his claim to being the best player in the league. One of his most breathtaking performances came during the season opener of the 2017–18 season. The Oilers were taking on their local rivals, the Calgary Flames. McDavid scored a hat trick in that game, but it was the second goal that had hockey fans everywhere buzzing.

With the Oilers up 1–0 in the third period, McDavid took the puck from one end of the ice to the other. Sportsnet tracked his speed. By the time McDavid had reached the far end of the ice, he was skating 25.1 mph (40.4 km/h). He blew past the Flames defenders as if they weren't there. Then he finished it by making a devastating move on goalie Mike Smith, cutting

McDavid celebrates his first-period goal against the Calgary Flames during the 2017–18 season opener.

sharply to the middle before flicking the puck over Smith's glove, for his second goal of the game.

Nobody plays the game as fast as McDavid can, which has helped him become such a dominant offensive player. "What he is able to do at his top speed, which is faster than anyone else's, is something I've never seen before," said Washington Capitals forward T. J. Oshie.

McDavid also became the first player in history to win the fastest skater event at the NHL All-Star Skills Competition twice, having won it in 2017 and 2018. In fact, the NHL had a hard time getting players to sign up for the 2018 fastest skater event because no one wanted to go head-to-head with McDavid.

Yet even as the spotlight shines brightly on McDavid, he remains humble and modest. From the time he was able to put on skates, he's been on a track to this superstardom. He lived up to that hype right away. In July 2017, McDavid signed a massive eight-year contract worth $100 million to stay with the Oilers. It also made him the highest-paid player in the NHL at just 21 years old. For McDavid, this is only the beginning of a dream come true.

"This is something I've been wanting to do since I was very, very young," McDavid said in 2017. "I can't say I expected this (early success), but you're working toward it and hoping for it. It's definitely something I've dreamt of."

CONNOR McDAVID AT-A-GLANCE

BIRTHPLACE: Richmond Hill, Ontario
BIRTH DATE: January 13, 1997
POSITION: Center
SHOOTS: Left
SIZE: 6'4", 192 pounds
TEAM: Edmonton Oilers
PREVIOUS TEAM: Erie Otters (OHL) (2012–15)
DRAFTED BY THE OILERS FIRST OVERALL IN 2015

CHAPTER 13

MATT MURRAY

Matt Murray is always going to have an interesting piece of trivia tied to his hockey career. Thanks to a quirk in the NHL rules and some pretty lucky timing, Murray is the only goaltender in NHL history to win two Stanley Cups as a rookie.

Wait, can't you be a rookie only once? Well, it would seem so. But the NHL has some rules about who is actually considered a rookie. One rule says if a player enters a season with 25 or fewer regular-season games under his belt, or five or fewer over the previous two seasons, then he is a rookie for that entire season. Rookies also must be 25 or younger.

In his first year with the Pittsburgh Penguins, Murray played in only 13 regular-season games. Then he went on a magical run during the playoffs,

Though in his early 20s, Matt Murray led the Penguins to back-to-back Stanley Cup championships.

Murray emerged in the 2016 playoffs as a goalie capable of leading his team to a championship.

surprising everyone by backstopping the Penguins to the 2016 Stanley Cup. But because he had played fewer than 26 games, he officially entered the next season as a rookie. So when he went ahead and took

the Penguins right back to the Cup in 2017, Murray became the first rookie goalie to have two Stanley Cups. It's a pretty impressive accomplishment to have on your résumé, that's for sure.

Murray turned 22 years old during that first Stanley Cup run. That made him one of the youngest and least-experienced goalies to win the Cup. It takes a pretty special individual to come into the most pressure-packed situation that hockey offers and play as well as Murray did. What made it even more impressive is that he did it twice. The last team to win back-to-back Stanley Cups had been the Detroit Red Wings way back in 1997 and 1998.

MURRAY'S FIRST "STANLEY CUP"

Before Murray led the Penguins to two consecutive Stanley Cups, he lifted an eight-inch replica made out of aluminum foil. As a kid Murray had made it for his father, James, for Father's Day. When Matt brought home the real Stanley Cup for his dad, James pulled out the little replica and the two were photographed holding their Stanley Cups together. James died in January 2018 following a sudden illness. After taking some time away from the team to be with his family during that difficult time, Murray took comfort in playing again. "Hockey definitely took a back seat for a couple days, but when you're out (on the ice), it's kind of a sanctuary," Murray said.

"I think Matt has always played his best," Penguins coach Mike Sullivan said, "when the pressure is on and the stakes are high."

Calmness under pressure is a huge benefit to any goaltender. The goalie is the only player on the ice for all 60 minutes of a game. He sometimes sees upwards of 40 shots during that time. Not only that, but a goalie has to react to the shots that don't even hit the net. It's a lot of movement, with very few breaks. That can mentally wear on individuals. A lot of goalie coaches will tell you that the mental part of goaltending is just as important, if not more so, than the physical side. Murray has always been very good at controlling his emotions and keeping his focus.

> **"I THINK MATT HAS ALWAYS PLAYED HIS BEST WHEN THE PRESSURE IS ON AND THE STAKES ARE HIGH."**
>
> –PENGUINS COACH MIKE SULLIVAN

"I have no expectations when I'm out there," Murray said after one of his many playoff wins. "I can't predict the future. I can't control most of what happens. All I can control is what I do."

Murray also had the added pressure of replacing one of the Penguins' most popular players. Marc-Andre Fleury had already backstopped the team to the 2009 Stanley Cup. But an injury at the start of the 2016 playoffs opened the door for Murray. The youngster played so well in Fleury's absence that he kept the starting job even after Fleury got healthy.

Fleury ended up moving on from the Penguins after the 2016–17 season. That made Murray the team's primary starter. The two Penguins goalies shared a special moment on the ice during the 2017 Stanley Cup celebration, though. Fleury was given the Cup to skate around with. He made a point to be the one to pass the Cup to Murray after another job well done by the youngster. It was kind of like he was passing the torch to Murray.

"I think we did a good job together to win this Cup," said Fleury, who appeared in 15 games during the 2017 Stanley Cup Playoffs when Murray was out with injury. "Matt is the goalie of the future for this team, I think it was important for him to celebrate tonight."

Murray was so touched by the gesture that it nearly brought him to tears. Even though they were competing for ice time, Murray had great respect for the veteran.

"He's been a really important mentor for me, just such a support person for me over the last couple of years," Murray said. "There's no way I'm able to play as freely as I do without it (Fleury) being there to support me. He's meant everything to me."

Now that Fleury is gone, it's all on Murray. After winning two Stanley Cups before he even reached veteran status in the league, the expectations are going to be even higher. But as Murray has shown in the very short time he's been in the NHL, he can handle just about anything that comes his way.

MATT MURRAY AT-A-GLANCE

BIRTHPLACE: Thunder Bay, Ontario
BIRTH DATE: May 25, 1994
POSITION: Goaltender
CATCHES: Left
SIZE: 6'4", 178 pounds
TEAM: Pittsburgh Penguins
PREVIOUS TEAMS: Sault Ste. Marie Greyhounds (OHL) (2010–14), Wilkes-Barre/Scranton Penguins (AHL) (2014–16)
DRAFTED BY THE PENGUINS 83RD OVERALL IN 2012

CHAPTER 14

DAVID PASTRNAK

When the Boston Bruins called David Pastrnak's name at the 2014 NHL Entry Draft, the Czech-born winger stood up, kissed both his hands, and pointed to the sky. Then he hugged his mother, who had already collapsed into tears. While those tears were mostly of joy, they were also tinged with sadness because of who couldn't be there that night.

A year before Boston took Pastrnak with the 25th selection in that draft, his father and coach Milan passed away after a battle with cancer. David was only four days shy of his 17th birthday when he lost his father. It was a crushing moment for him and his family. But Pastrnak always carried his father's memory and the lessons Milan Pastrnak taught with him as he continued on in his career.

David Pastrnak was ready to contribute on a winning team when the Boston Bruins drafted him in 2014.

Right after Pastrnak signed his first contract with the Bruins, he said the person he thought of most—just as he did on his draft night—was his father.

"I've been always just dreaming about it," Pastrnak said of signing his first NHL contract. "Now it's come true, but my dreaming isn't done. I have to still do more things for my dad, and for my family."

> **"I'VE BEEN ALWAYS JUST DREAMING ABOUT IT. NOW IT'S COME TRUE, BUT MY DREAMING ISN'T DONE."**
>
> **–DAVID PASTRNAK**

Only 18 years old, Pastrnak was already a mature person for his age. He had left home at 16 to play professionally in Sweden's second division. While he was there, the Bruins noticed just how talented he was. In particular, they marveled at his puck skills. When he got going, Pastrnak could make defenders look foolish.

Still, scouts didn't consider Pastrnak to be among the top prospects. Although he ended up being picked in the first round of the NHL draft, he soon showed that he probably should have been drafted a lot higher.

The Bruins started Pastrnak with their minor league team, the Providence Bruins. He quickly showed he was ready for the big show. Less than a year after he was drafted, Pastrnak was an NHL player. Many of those players drafted ahead of him still toiled in the minors.

Pastrnak's puck-handling and playmaking ability stood out right away during his rookie season. By his third year in the league, he was no longer an unknown or underrated player. That 2016–17 season was a breakout year for Pastrnak, who became one of the most dangerous wingers in the NHL. He scored 34 goals that year, putting him in the league's top 10 at only 20 years old.

Between 2005–06 and 2017–18, only four players scored more goals than Pastrnak by the time they were 21 years old. That group consisted of Steven Stamkos, Sidney Crosby, Alex Ovechkin, and Jeff Skinner. Three of them went on to win goal-scoring titles in their careers. Needless to say, that was pretty impressive company for Pastrnak.

One reason Pastrnak thrived in the NHL was that he fit in well among great players. At various points in his Bruins career, he's played on a line with Patrice Bergeron and Brad Marchand. Bergeron is one of the best two-way centers in the game. Marchand has

Pastrnak had six goals and 14 assists in 12 games during the
2018 playoffs.

gone from a super-pest who annoys his opponents to a super-pest who can score in bunches. And when Pastrnak has played with those two, it's been magic on ice. Many considered them one of the best lines in the entire NHL.

Bergeron has played with and against the best players in the world, but he has shown a lot of respect for his young teammate. During the 2018 playoffs, the Bruins' veteran raved about Pastrnak.

> "HE'S GOT THAT CONFIDENCE, BUT HE ALSO WANTS TO BE THE GUY. HE WANTS TO MAKE THOSE PLAYS. IF HE DOESN'T HAVE THE PUCK, HE WANTS IT BACK. THAT'S WHAT AMAZES ME WITH HIM."
>
> –PATRICE BERGERON

"He's got that confidence, but he also wants to be the guy," Bergeron said. "He wants to make those plays. If he doesn't have the puck, he wants it back. That's what amazes me with him. There are a lot of skill players who are great when they have the puck, and when they don't have it, they don't necessarily want it back as much as this guy. We talk a lot about it, but we learn just as much playing with him as he does playing with us."

The excitement that Pastrnak, or "Pasta," as fans and teammates call him, brings the to the ice every shift is the reason people buy tickets to watch hockey. One of his best goals came early in the 2017–18 season against the Vancouver Canucks. He took the puck from behind the Bruins net and showed what happens when you give him room to pick up speed.

Pastrnak started in his own zone. He darted around Canucks forward Markus Granlund, who could only helplessly wave his stick at him. Then he picked up speed through the neutral zone, blew past another Canucks forward, and went one-on-one

FROM IDOL TO TEAMMATE

Growing up in the Czech Republic, Pastrnak's favorite player was fellow Czech star David Krejci. The Bruins had drafted Krejci 10 years prior to taking Pastrnak. When Pastrnak was drafted, his countryman reached out. "It was unreal, you know. (As) a kid, you have an idol who you're looking for, and then one day he just writes a message, so I felt really good," Pastrnak said.

with Vancouver defenseman Michael Del Zotto. Now at a blazing pace, Pastrnak slipped the puck under Del Zotto, cut to the middle, and before the other defenseman, Ben Hutton, could even get a stick on him, Pastrnak chipped the puck through goalie Anders Nilsson for a goal. It stood as one of the season's very best.

It was a great example of the immense talent Pastrnak possesses and why he has become one of the most electrifying young forwards in the league.

DAVID PASTRNAK AT-A-GLANCE

BIRTHPLACE: Havirov, Czech Republic
BIRTH DATE: May 25, 1996
POSITION: Right Wing
SHOOTS: Right
SIZE: 6', 188 pounds
TEAM: Boston Bruins
PREVIOUS TEAM: Södertälje (SHL)
DRAFTED BY THE BRUINS 25TH OVERALL IN 2014

CHAPTER 15

MARK SCHEIFELE

May 31, 2011, was a day for celebration in Winnipeg. Fifteen years after the beloved Jets moved to Arizona and became the Coyotes, NHL hockey was coming back to Manitoba. On this day, the league announced the Atlanta Thrashers would relocate to Winnipeg ahead of the coming season.

Just having a team was a relief to fans. Yet that was only the beginning. A few weeks later, team officials were down the road in St. Paul, Minnesota, for the NHL draft. While there, the team would not only select its first new player of the Winnipeg era but also announce its new name. The excitement was palpable in the building as many people from Winnipeg made the trip to witness this bit of history.

As the newly relocated Winnipeg Jets' first draft pick, Mark Scheifele had big expectations to live up to.

Rumors circulated as to what the name might be. Many fans had a clear preference. Then the moment came. New owner Mark Chipman stepped up to the microphone on the draft stage. He introduced the team's new general manager, Kevin Cheveldayoff, who was to make the seventh overall pick. Chipman began to make the pick: "On behalf of the Winnipeg Jets."

The crowd roared with approval. Winnipeg fans never wanted the Jets to leave, and now they were thrilled to have a new Jets team. When the crowd died down, Cheveldayoff continued: "The Winnipeg Jets are proud to select, from the Barrie Colts of the OHL, Mark Scheifele."

That made the Ontario-born Scheifele the first pick in the new Winnipeg Jets' history. It was a time of hope and optimism in Winnipeg. They had their name back, and now they had a top young prospect. Now that player just needed to perform.

Some players might have felt burdened by that pressure. Scheifele, on the other hand, was used to facing long odds. He had been a bit of an underdog for much of his young career.

Scheifele played junior hockey in the OHL. But when he first joined that league, his name wasn't called until the seventh round of the OHL draft. Some scouts viewed him as too small, whereas others judged him simply not good enough to play at that level. But as it turned out, Scheifele was just a bit of a late bloomer. By the time he reached the NHL, he stood 6-foot-3 and weighted more than 200 pounds.

Still, the road was not easy. The Jets gave Scheifele a chance to make their team out of training camp right after his draft year. He made the roster, but after seven games the Jets believed he wasn't quite ready to play at that level. They sent him back to Barrie to

IT TAKES A JET TO TEACH A JET

Maybe it was coincidence, or maybe it was fate, but Scheifele had one of the best teachers he could have asked for prior to becoming a full-time Jet. Playing for the Barrie Colts in the OHL, Scheifele's coach was Dale Hawerchuk. Hawerchuk had played nine seasons for the original Jets and is widely considered the best player to throw on a Winnipeg uniform. The Hockey Hall of Famer made a huge impression on Scheifele as a younger player. "He's just a wealth of knowledge," Scheifele said. "He went through so many experiences in his career and was able to pass on a lot of knowledge to me. He was a big mentor of mine."

play another year in the OHL. Most 18-year-olds aren't ready for that kind of responsibility anyway.

The team gave him another chance at the NHL level the next year, too. But this time Scheifele lasted only four games before the Jets decided to once again send him back to juniors. Fans were growing a bit restless. Wasn't this kid supposed to be their star?

Scheifele didn't let the demotions get him down. He still had a lot of work to do, but slowly he started putting more and more together. The growing center had a decent rookie season in 2013–14, and he looked a little better the next year. Then, in 2015–16, everything started to click for the young forward.

Scheifele put up 29 goals in 71 games and suddenly started to look more like the guy the Jets took seventh overall back in 2011. The next fall he was named to Team North America for the 2016 World Cup of Hockey, playing alongside the game's best Canadian and American players 23 and younger. The coaching staff there liked Scheifele so much that they put him on the team's top line with Connor McDavid and Auston Matthews. Those two had just gone No. 1 overall in back-to-back drafts. Together, the top line gave opponents fits with their speed and skill.

It turned out that Scheifele was just getting warmed up. He continued getting better and better. He also was getting faster, which is something teammate and captain Blake Wheeler noticed right away. It inspired Wheeler to start working even harder on his own game.

"I just knew there was more there, and watching the progression Sheif made, a light went off for me that I can get better," Wheeler said. "I think as long as you have that mind-set, no matter how old you are, you can keep improving every year."

That's the kind of mind-set Scheifele always has had, even when times were tough and people started to wonder if he might be a draft bust instead of the budding star he became.

"There's nobody that invests in themselves more than Mark Scheifele in the NHL," Wheeler said. "There's not an outlet that he hasn't reached out to. There's not a trick he hasn't tried. So for me playing with him, I've got to try to keep up, right?"

Part of what makes Scheifele so good at improving himself is that he's widely known as one of the best students of the game. It comes from a place of deep passion for the sport, one that Scheifele is proud to

Scheifele's commitment to improving his game has helped the Jets rise in the standings and become a contender.

share with anyone. He's always watching others to see how those skills can translate to his own game.

"There are a lot of guys in the league who will tell you, 'I like to leave it all at the rink. I don't watch much hockey when I get home. Yeah, that's definitely not me,'" Scheifele wrote in *The Players' Tribune*. "I'm what you might call a full-on hockey nerd. I can watch hockey all day. Like, when we're headed to the airport after a game, I'll pull out my phone right on the bus and just start streaming the late games. I'm always fascinated by why guys are playing a certain way, or taking chances in certain moments, or adding little tricks to their game. You watch any hockey game closely enough, and there's going to be something you can pick up."

It took a lot of patience and a lot of work for Scheifele to get to where he is now. He is widely considered one of the very best young centers in the game and has proven the Jets right for making him the first player to restart their franchise with.

MARK SCHEIFELE AT-A-GLANCE

BIRTHPLACE: Kitchener, Ontario
BIRTH DATE: March 15, 1993
POSITION: Center
SHOOTS: Right
SIZE: 6'3", 207 pounds
TEAM: Winnipeg Jets
PREVIOUS TEAM: Barrie Colts (OHL) (2010–13)
DRAFTED BY THE JETS SEVENTH OVERALL IN 2011

ROOKIE RECORDS

MOST GOALS

1. Teemu Selanne, Winnipeg Jets (1992–93): 76
2. Mike Bossy, New York Islanders (1977–78): 53
3. Alex Ovechkin, Washington Capitals (2005–06): 52

MOST ASSISTS

1. Wayne Gretzky, Edmonton Oilers (1979–80): 86
2. Joe Juneau, Boston Bruins (1992–93): 70
3. Peter Stastny, Quebec Nordiques (1980–81): 70

SCORING BY A DEFENSEMAN

1. Mark Howe, Hartford Whalers (1979–80): 80
2. Larry Murphy, Los Angeles Kings (1980–81): 76
3. Brian Leetch, New York Rangers (1988–89): 71

GOALIE WINS

1. Terry Sawchuk, Detroit Red Wings (1950–51): 44
2. Ed Belfour, Chicago Blackhawks (1990–91): 43
3. Roger Crozier, Detroit Red Wings (1964–65): 40

Accurate as of the start of the 2018–19 season

NEW WAVE DREAM TEAM

What might a dream team of players born in 1994 or later look like? Here's what the author says.

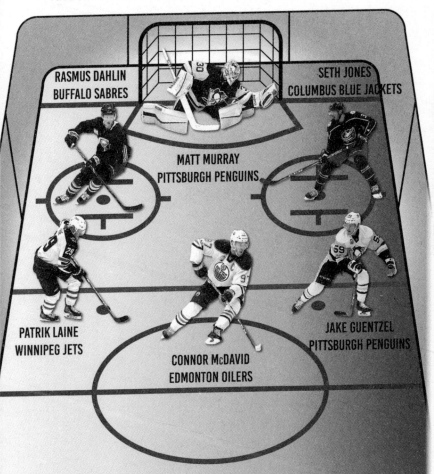

RASMUS DAHLIN
BUFFALO SABRES

SETH JONES
COLUMBUS BLUE JACKETS

MATT MURRAY
PITTSBURGH PENGUINS

PATRIK LAINE
WINNIPEG JETS

JAKE GUENTZEL
PITTSBURGH PENGUINS

CONNOR McDAVID
EDMONTON OILERS

FOR MORE INFORMATION

BOOKS

Gretzky, Wayne, and Kirstie McLellan Day. 99: *Stories of the Game.* New York: G. P. Putnam's Sons, 2016.

Peters, Chris. *Hockey Season Ticket: The Ultimate Fan Guide.* Mendota Heights, MN: Press Box Books, 2018.

Sports Illustrated: The Hockey Book. New York: Sports Illustrated Books, 2010.

ON THE WEB

Elite Prospects
www.eliteprospects.com

Hockey Reference
www.hockey-reference.com

National Hockey League
www.nhl.com

PLACES TO VISIT

Hockey Hall of Fame
30 Yonge St.
Toronto, ON M5E 1X8
416-360-7735
www.hhof.com

Learn about the history of the game and the greatest players of all time at the museum in downtown Toronto. Interactive exhibits bring fans closer to the action, and fans can also get an up-close look at the Stanley Cup.

United States Hockey Hall of Fame
801 Hat Trick Ave.
Eveleth, MN 55734
800-443-7825
www.ushockeyhall.com

The history of American hockey is on display at this museum in northern Minnesota. In addition to learning about top US players, visitors can also watch footage of the historic 1980 Olympic team and test out their skills on a replica rink.

SELECT BIBLIOGRAPHY

Bombulie, Jonathan. "Penguins' Matt Murray Returns to 'Sanctuary' 6 Days After Dad's Death." *Trib Live*, 22 Jan. 2018, http://bit.ly/2n0KCWD.

"David Pastrnak's Major Impact on Boston Bruins." NBC *Sports*, www.nbcsports.com/video/david-pastrnak-honors-his-late-father-major-impact-boston-bruins. Accessed 3 Aug. 2018.

Gilbertson, Wes. "'Who Is This Kid?!': Flames Scout Knew Right Away Gaudreau Had Star Potential." *Calgary Sun*, 26 Jan. 2018, www.calgarysun.com/sports/hockey/nhl/calgary-flames/who-is-this-kid-flames-scout-knew-right-away-gaudreau-would-be-a-star/.

Guentzel, Jake. "Kesselmania Runs Wild." *The Players' Tribune*, 12 May 2017, www.theplayerstribune.com/en-us/articles/jake-guentzel-kesselmania-runs-wild.

Hoppe, Bill. "The Young and the Restless." *USA Hockey Magazine*, Dec. 2017, www.usahockeymagazine.com/article/2017-12/young-and-restless.

McKenzie, Bob. *Hockey Confidential: Inside Stories from the People inside the Game.* Toronto: Collins, 2014.

Mirtle, James. "How Auston Matthews Became Hockey's Hottest Prospect." *The Globe and Mail,* 20 June 2016, www.theglobeandmail.com/sports/hockey/why-everyone-in-hockey-is-talking-about-auston-matthews-toronto-maple-leafs/article30508528/.

Prewitt, Alex. "The Arrival: Connor McDavid's Ascension Was Guided by the Forces of NHL Greatness." *Sports Illustrated,* 5 March 2017, www.si.com/nhl/2017/03/05/connor-mcdavid-oilers-sidney-crosby-bobby-orr.

Spencer, Donna. "Jets Great Dale Hawerchuk Enjoying Protege Mark Scheifele's Success." *CBC,* 16 May 2018, www.cbc.ca/sports/hockey/nhl/mark-scheifele-dale-hawerchuk-winnipeg-jets-1.4666381.

Wyshynski, Greg. "Chara a Towering Influence on Young Bruins Blueliners." *ESPN,* 20 Nov. 2017, www.espn.com/nhl/story/_/id/21487102.

INDEX

ABOUT THE AUTHOR

Chris Peters is the NHL Draft and prospects analyst for ESPN.com. Peters has covered the NHL since 2012 and has written four previous children's books on hockey. Prior to joining ESPN, Peters wrote for CBSSports.com, NCAA.com, USA *Hockey Magazine*, and USAHockey.com, and he was the founding editor of the popular blog, United States of Hockey. He resides in North Liberty, Iowa, with his wife and two children.